THE POETRY OF EZRA POUND

I.

THE POETRY OF
EZRA POUND

BY

ALICE STEINER AMDUR

NEW YORK / RUSSELL & RUSSELL

PREFACE

Ezra Pound first appealed to me as a challenge. I could not reconcile the apparent
confusion and meaninglessness of the *Cantos*
with the fact that it is impossible to keep
Pound's name out of any discussion of modern poetry, and that T. S. Eliot has termed
the *Cantos* themselves the only "poem of
some length" by a contemporary that he can
read with enjoyment and admiration.[1]

I therefore undertook a study of the development of Pound's poetry, as shown in the
poetry itself and further illuminated by his
prose. Surprised at first by the disparity between his exquisite early lyrics and the tur-
bulent cantos, I now feel that they do cohere.
I see the development of Ezra Pound as the
story of a man with an extraordinary flair for
language and music who, after achieving
mastery in a certain type of lyric and translation, deserted the field of pure art to cam-
paign for a variety of other causes, and has
buried his poetry beneath an ever growing
mass of propaganda.

Since there has been no biography of
Pound, nor any comprehensive study of his
poetry, I have had to rely almost exclusively
on his writing for my understanding of the
poet's development. The notable exception
has been the comment of T. S. Eliot, which,
always enlightening, often makes Pound appear at once more clear and more profound
than Pound argues himself.

I am greatly indebted to my tutor, Dr.
Theodore Spencer, who has told me what he
knows of Pound, and to Mr. James Laughlin IV, who, through his personal friendship
with Pound, has given me a more intimate
picture of the man than I could otherwise
have acquired.

A. S. A.

THE POETRY OF EZRA POUND

I
THE BACKGROUND: AMERICA AND
THE POET

W HEN Ezra Pound left America in 1908 he
was leaving a country where most people who
felt at all about poetry felt that if Americans
could not write like Longfellow, Emerson,
Whitman, or Whittier, they could at least
try. "There was no one in America" Pound
wrote later, "whose work was of the slightest
interest for a serious artist." [2] *Poems for
Travelers, Birds of the Poets, Patriotic Poems
of New Jersey, Poets on Christmas* were typical anthologies published that year, and of
the few individual poets to offer their wares
to the public, not one was even second rate.
America had no longer any literary capital,
and as a province of England received in
much diluted form what the English Mrs.
Grundy called art. As Pound states it, the
spreading of knowledge was as follows:

When a brilliant person or a specialist in London gets tired of a set of ideas . . . or when he
happens to need the money, he refrigerates the

[9]

ideas into a book. And the London reviewers and journalists review it, and absorb some of the ideas and dilute them to ten per cent. of the original force. And the American Press dilutes the result to ten per cent. of the derivative strength, and the American public gets the "hogwash." And if you try to talk on any such exotic matters with Americans, you get the hogwash.

And if you have any vital interest in arts and happen to like talking about them, you sooner or later leave the country.[3]

This, like almost all of Pound's propaganda prose, is an exaggeration, but as an exaggeration of a truth it indicates both the country and the man. For years writers of the East had feebly echoed their Tennyson and, with nothing to say, had chosen exigent forms and stuffed them with clichés, while in the West "red blood" poetry had faded to an uncertain pink. Of course ever since 1880 some few men had felt the limitations of the Anglo-American tradition, even when this tradition included Browning and Yeats as well as Tennyson and Swinburne. The American Mrs. Grundy had been so prejudiced against France that a reaction was inevitable, and returning expatriates smuggled in knowledge of Gautier, Verlaine, and Baudelaire. But for a long time the literature of France was a Bohemian challenge rather than a serious study; even Hovey and Carman, for all their interest in certain Symbolist doctrines, were not really convinced of the importance of technical study.

The year 1908 was really a lull between two generations; there was excitement under the surface but outwardly the poetry was well characterized as "seeds in a dry pod, tick, tick, tick." Pound felt that this deadness in poetry was a mark of general lethargy in American culture. With two college degrees and four months of teaching experience, he was, at the age of twenty-three, convinced that American education was a "dead and uncorrelated system" where very few people knew what "comparative literature" meant or approached it with a "considered, conscious method." [4] He had begun an examination of comparative literature in or about 1901 [5]; theoretically it meant for him "a literary scholarship which will weigh Theocritus and Mr. Yeats with one balance, and which will judge dull dead men as inexorably as dull writers of today, and will, with equity, give praise to beauty before referring to an almanack." [6] But his own study of comparative literature came to concentrate, as we shall see, on extracting from previous ages certain technical lessons which his own age needed and which his genius was qualified to transmit.

Pound was born with an exquisitely perceptive ear, and he cultivated an exact sense of language. The first period to which he applied these gifts was that hundred years in pre-renaissance Europe during which the troubadours composed their finest songs, and when Guido Cavalcanti and Dante gave a direction to the Italian language. For this study he was armed, of necessity, with a knowledge of French, Italian, and Provençal. He knew Spanish as well; in fact it was a proposed study of Lope de Vega that sent him to Europe in 1906, but "After work in Spain and Italy, after pursuing the Provençal verb from Milan to Freiburg, he deserted the thesis on Lope de Vega, and the Ph.D. and the professorial chair, and elected to remain in Europe." [7] Since 1908 he has never returned.

In fleeing from twentieth century America to twelfth century Provence, Pound was making a romantic escape in appearance only. He admitted that some temperamental sympathy might have prejudiced him in favor of this age,[8] but his sympathy was no desire to "fade far away." On the contrary, he came to the canzoni of Arnaut Daniel deliberately seeking a literary discipline, "seeing that they satisfy not only the modern ear, gluttonous of rhyme, but also the ear trained to Roman and Hellenic music, to which rhyme seemed and seems a vulgarity." [9] By entering a new age Pound thought he had thrown off the past of his own language. "I fly on the wings of an unknown chord," he proclaims:

> That ye hear not,
>   Can not discern
> My music is wierd and untaméd
> Barbarous, wild, extreme . . .
> And lo, your outworn harmonies are behind me
>   As ashes and mouldy bread.[10]

This is a bold and invigorating statement, but in the very next stanza Pound shows us that his desire to shake off the past has anticipated his emancipation.

> My joy is the wind of heaven
>   My drink is the gall of night
> My love is the light of meteors
>   The autumn leaves in flight

are lines which any young man of the day might have written, and compose one of the least true assertions Pound ever made about himself. Neither early nor late was he, poetically, interested in the wind of heaven or the light of meteors; it was precisely against such loose appeal to the elements and invocation of general terms to stir up vague emotions that Pound was in revolt. This poem is not in his collected edition.

Swinburne and "the nineties" were present somewhere in the back of Pound's mind when he wrote his first poems. He was naturally impressed by Swinburne's elastic use of verse forms, even if he did rebel as early as 1906 against his

> Entangled music that men may not
> Over readily understand.[11]

It is difficult to distinguish the element of genuine revivification of Provence, as Eliot has suggested, from the element of romantic fantasy which Pound acquired from the nineties, and which was present in disguise in his early poems.[12] This is clear enough if we compare any Provençal poem from Pound's first book with a poem written on the same subject after he learned the value of the chiseled phrase.

But if Swinburne and the nineties were in the background, Browning and Yeats were very much in the foreground of Pound's mind; they were probably the best masters he could find in his own language, but his first enthusiasm merely took the form of imitation:

Here's to you, Old Hippety-Hop o' the accents,
True to the Truth's sake and crafty dissector,
You grabbed at the gold sure; had no need to pack
    cents
Into your versicles.
                Clear sight's elector! [13]

This is healthy imitation on the side of parody. Pound's imitation of Yeats is more dangerous than this tribute to Browning, because it is less conscious:

    For I was a gaunt, grave councillor
    Being in all things wise, and very old,
    But I have put aside this folly and the cold
    That old age weareth for a cloak.[14]

II

PROVENCE: THE LITERARY
IMPACT

It was to escape such superficial word-resemblances and to get at the cadence of poetry that Pound studied poets of a different age and tradition. Convinced that "Poets who will not study music are defective," [15] and that "Any study of European poetry is unsound if it does not commence with a study of that art in Provence," [16] Pound learned all there was to learn from a poetry that is nearer music than literature.

According to his own later accounts, he learned from Arnaut Daniel that "the music of rhymes depends on their arrangement, not on their multiplicity," [17] and he learned from him too "an aesthetic of sound; of clear sounds and opaque sounds, such as *Sols sui*, an opaque sound like Swinburne at his best; and in *Doutz brais* and in *L'aura amara* a clear sound with staccato; and of heavy beats and of running and light beats. . . ." [18] Pound studied Daniel more closely than any other troubadour; he may well have seen the early poet as a prototype of himself. Daniel,

who also had "left learning to become a
jongleur" wrote in Provence "between 1180
and 1200 . . . when the Provençal was growing weary, and it was to be seen if it could
last, and he tried to make almost a new language, or at least to enlarge the Langue d'Oc,
and make new things possible." [19] He did
this by introducing unusual rime words, and
using them in new combinations, and by using, always, "the picturesque verb with an
exact meaning." [20]

From Bertran de Born, Piere Vidal, and
Arnaut of Marvoil, as well as from Daniel,
Pound learned new structures and new cadences, and we see him practicing them all in
his first book.[21] He does not discard the sonnet, and he even plays with the heroic coup-
let, but in the one form he continually varies
the sestet, and in the other he experiments
with anapests to speed up the tempo.

His entire interest in *A Lume Spento* lies
in studying the value of words as music, as
opposed to words as oratory: he experiments
incessantly with meters and rimes until he
can get just the tempo and the harmony that
makes each poem a song. The preponder-
ance of dactylic and trochaic lines over iam-

[17]

bic in the early poems — a mannerism that comes possibly from Browning, probably from the troubadours themselves — gives a restlessness and vigor that center attention on the beginning of the line rather than on the rime word. But with his rimes Pound does wonderful things; he makes some echo from stanza to stanza, and others he never resolves; with some words he will build up a melodic refrain, and with others he will cut the melody like a knife. We see something of his skill in "Na Audiart."

> Though thou well dost wish me ill
> > Audiart, Audiart,
> Where thy bodice laces start
> As ivy fingers clutching through
> Its crevices,
> > Audiart, Audiart,
> Stately, tall and lovely tender
> Who shall render
> > Audiart, Audiart,
> Praises meet unto thy fashion?
> Here a word kiss!
> > Pass I on.

A little later the tune changes:

> Bespeak thyself for anything.
> Just a word in thy praise, girl,
> Just for the swirl
> Thy satins make upon the stair.

This almost sounds like Browning, not "Old Hippety-Hop o' the accents" but the Browning who first taught Pound to concentrate on the kernel of thought and the word to express it, the Browning who helped Pound slough off "the nineties," and who is to stay with him in the journey from Provence to London. In "Cino" we see a different aspect of his influence. Pound has taken Browning's dramatic monologue,

> Bah! I have sung women in three cities,
> But it is all the same;
> And I will sing of the sun,

but he has not yet made it his own. Once Pound had tried this form he could not relinquish it; he recognized here the perfect medium through which to express his vivid sense of the past, and ever since he has done much of his best work in the monologue. But he was still experimenting, and he found he could render more than one mood — age and weariness as well as the youth and gaiety of "Cino." "In Tempus Senectus" [22] is a study in which each line is the breath of an old man, and each phrase requires a new effort of speech. But it achieves this effect only because Pound has used such skill in

interposing his sad, short refrain "For we
are old" between longer lines that fade away
with the weak feminine endings "dieth,"
"crieth," "flieth." These first poems show
a genuine poetic impulse which I think
Pound has never expressed more charmingly
than in the opening stanzas of his "Praise of
Ysolt":

In vain have I striven,
            to teach my heart to bow;
In vain have I said to him
"There be many singers greater than thou."

But his answer cometh, as winds and as lutany,
As a vague crying upon the night
That leaveth me no rest, saying ever,
            "Song, a song."

Their echoes play upon each other in the twilight
Seeking ever a song.
Lo, I am worn with travail
And the wandering of many roads hath made my
      eyes
As dark red circles filled with dust.
Yet there is a trembling upon me in the twilight,
    And little red elf words crying "A song,"
    Little grey elf words crying for a song,
    Little brown leaf words crying "A song,"
    Little green leaf words crying for a song.
The words are as leaves, old brown leaves in the
      spring time
Blowing they know not whither, seeking a song.

III

LONDON: PUBLICATIONS AND
PEOPLE

With the little money he gathered from
the publication of this first volume, and after
he had been abroad only five months, Pound
went up to London, still seeking "such as
love this same beauty that I love somewhat
after mine own fashion." [23] In particular he
sought William Butler Yeats, his only living
master. When they met in London Yeats's
poetry was changing; he too was throwing
off the past. No longer did he supply Pound
with an attitude and a vocabulary; his true
and permanent influence, as both poets ma-
tured, lay in giving Pound the example of a
poet with a vivid imagination who spent all
his life stripping off layers of rhetoric.

Pound was working hard on his Provençal,
French, and Italian poems. With some new
ones and some written much earlier but not
included in *A Lume Spento* [24] he sought Elkin
Mathews, the publisher. Mathews was much
impressed by the poems, but wanted Pound
to help pay the expenses of publishing something so new and daring. Pound had, and

offered, a shilling — and Mathews published.[25] Their strange original quality was
recognized instantly by a certain group, and
even the *Daily News* was enthusiastic. The
new title, *Personae*, was happy: taken from
the Latin, it means "Masks of the Actor,"
and his use of it showed that Pound had already recognized his *genre*. The most important of the new poems join the class initi-
ated by "Cino," which used the monologue
to present a character and a situation.
"Marvoil," in brusque and unadorned free
verse, tells the story of Arnaut the Less.

Aragon cursing in Aragon, Beziers busy at
    Beziers —
Bored to an inch of extinction,
Tibors all tongue and temper at Mont-Ausier,
Me! in this damn'd inn of Avignon,
Stringing long verse for the Burlatz;
All for one half-bald, knock-knee'd king of the
    Aragonese,
Alfonso, Quattro, poke-nose.

This is not better music than the old "Little
brown leaf words crying 'A song'" or the
new and lovely "White Stag," but it is a
vivid pouring of Pound into Marvoil, and
shows that Pound's *Personae*, although de-

[22]

scended from Browning's *Men and Women*, now speak with an original accent.

The "Idyll for Glaucus" [26] I find, despite Eliot's praise, weakly sentimental; it is no more successful than Leigh Hunt's *Rimini* in expanding Dante. But fortunately Pound already had strong hints that his genius lay in compression rather than diffuseness.

Aside from Yeats, cultural England had seemed to Pound as dreary a waste as cultural America, but six days after the appearance of *Personae* he met a group of young people as firmly opposed as he was to "that doddard Palgrave" and the system that supported him. T. E. Hulme was the leader, and his "Autumn," one of the first "Imagist" poems, had already appeared. Around him he gathered Edward Storer, F. S. Flint, F. W. Tancred, Joseph Campbell, Miss Florence Farr, and one or two others. Flint had been advocating a poetry in *vers libre* akin to the Japanese, "to which an image is the resonant heart of an exquisite moment." The new group, as Flint describes it,

proposed at various times to replace it [conventional verse forms] by pure *vers libre*, by the Japanese *tanka* and *haikai*; we all wrote dozens of

THE POETRY OF EZRA POUND

the latter as an amusement; by poems of a sacred Hebrew form, of which "This is the House that Jack Built" is a perfect model . . . by rhymeless poems like Hulme's "Autumn" and so on. In all this Hulme was the ringleader. He insisted too on absolutely accurate presentation and no verbiage; he and F. W. Tancred . . . used to spend hours each day in search for the right phrase. . . . There was also a lot of talk and practice among us, Storer leading it chiefly, of what we called the Image. We were very much interested in modern French symbolist poetry.[27]

Here at last Pound discovered people with whom he could discuss "such exotic matters" without getting the "hogwash." His own part in the discussion was at once modest and rather typical. Flint says of him in the same account:

Ezra Pound used to boast in those days that he was *Nil praeter 'Villon' et doctus cantare Catullum,* and he could not be made to believe that there was any French poetry after Ronsard. He was very full of his *troubadours*; but I do not remember that he did more than attempt to illustrate (or refute) our theories occasionally with their example.

And in a letter to Richard Aldington, Flint stated that "Pound added *nothing* to their meetings — absolutely nothing." [28] Pound

did, however, read them his new poem,
"Sestina: Altaforte," "whereupon the entire
café trembled." [29] I think this poem is sufficient justification, if any be needed, for
Pound's lingering in Provence. His manage-
ment of the intricate sestina, which he was
soon to describe as "a form like a thin sheet
of flame folding and infolding upon itself,"[30]
is a remarkable *tour de force* even though he
reverses his tags in the third and fourth lines
of the fourth stanza and then overlooks his
laxness. But this poem is more than a *tour
de force*, it is a "Persona," perhaps the most
insistently alive character in whom Pound
had yet masked himself. Dante put Bertran
de Born in Hell as a stirrer up of strife;
Pound has certainly brought him up again.
With equal vigor Pound brings up Piere
Vidal, the fool who ran mad as a wolf because of his love for Loba of Penautier. And
we have Bertran again, sorrowing for the
death of the young English king. The book
in which these poems appear (*Exultations*,
also published by Mathews in 1909) marks
Pound as fully established in his first manner. He can mask himself in the past and
through this medium render into English the

[25]

alba, canzon, sestina, ballade, and planh; he can also sing in the present. He has mastered the most intricate of all rime schemes, and then, in "Night Litany," tossed it aside to write an almost quantitative measure, of which Eliot has said "Such a 'freedom' as this lays so heavy a burden upon every word in a line that it becomes impossible to write like Shelley, leaving blanks for the adjectives, or like Swinburne, whose adjectives are practically blanks." [31]

But although he seemed to have learned their lesson, Pound could not say good-by to his troubadours, nor to Guido, Dante, and Villon. *The Spirit of Romance*, appearing in 1910, was his prose commentary on all his studies to date. A year later *Canzoni* appeared — more poems in the old manner. With but one or two exceptions these poems are interesting only for their technical proficiency. They seem to have been written for himself, because he loved medievalism and had lived so long in this atmosphere that half hints of action passed for life; they are certainly not written for a vulgar public which does not otherwise know, or care, about Provence. But Pound has never writ-

[26]

ten to please the vulgar public: he berates it when necessary, as we shall see later.

It was not only intoxication with the past that made Pound haunt old centuries; he wanted, above all, to free himself from "the crust of dead English," [32] and with a view to this he translated Guido Cavalcanti. The Italian sonnets and ballads were much less songs than those of Provence; "thought which in Provence had confined itself to the manner, now makes conquest of the matter of verse," [33] and in trying to render clearly Cavalcanti's introactive clauses Pound underwent a new and beneficial discipline which really marked a halfway stage between his appreciation of the word-as-music and the word-as-image.

Pound acknowledged Rossetti as both father and mother in these translations,[34] and the parentage is sufficiently obvious. One would expect Pound to be harder and more compact than Rossetti, but he still betrays a softness that may be a hangover from the nineties. Certainly the change in texture from "Thy form is more resplendent than sun's sheen" to the crisp thirty-sixth canto, "A Lady asks me," is not justified by a cor-

[27]

responding difference in the originals. Allowing for variance in mood and matter, there is hardly as much change in spirit from Cavalcanti's "Avete in voi li fiori, et la verdura" to his "Donna mi Priegha" [35] as the translations suggest.

IV

THE SCHOOL OF PRECISION

Except for the publication of these three
volumes of Pound, 1910 and 1911 were dead
years for poetry.[36] Hulme was now on the
continent; his club had died. But before
leaving London he had planted in Pound
seeds of imagism which he himself had derived from Remy de Gourmont.[37] Hulme
knew, as they all did, that there could be no
new flowering of verse until there was a new
technique. By "technique" he meant an
entirely new approach to writing. It was
essential, he thought, that poets should learn
to write about "small dry things"; accurate
description should be a legitimate object of
verse, and there should be no need to drag in
cosmic emotion. For this sort of poetry ex-
treme concentration was essential. A poet
could write about so slight a thing as the way
a woman's skirt rebounded from her heels,
*provided he noticed it with sufficient zest to
find the exact word to describe it.*[38] The hard,
definite, personal word was the essential:

It [poetry] is not a counter language, but a
visual concrete one. It is a compromise for a lan-

guage of intuition which would hand over sensation bodily. It always endeavours to arrest you, and to make you continuously see a physical thing, to prevent you gliding through an abstract process. It chooses fresh epithets and fresh metaphors not so much because they are new, and we are tired of the old, but because the old cease to convey a physical thing and become abstract counters. . . . Images in verse are not mere decoration, but the very essence of an intuitive language.[39]

This was the theory behind the Imagist poetry, and it came from France. But before reading any French literature written since the time of Ronsard, Pound had felt the necessity of seeking the right word, the *mot juste* in the French sense.

> Just for the swirl
> Thy satins make upon the stair

he had written some years before, the perfect example of Hulme's tumultuous petticoat. And in 1910 he had translated Daniel's "Mil vetz lo jorn en badaill em n'estendi"[40] by "A thousand times a day I yawn and stretch," adding in brackets "I give the most vigorous and perhaps brutal, though exact equivalent of two words which the euphuist would render 'languish' and 'yearn.'"[41] His deliberate archaisms (Fere, everychone), his straining of constructions (us-toward, her-ward), arise from the same desire to startle the reader by presenting a word or phrase which the subject demands but which the reader does not expect. Pound had not yet adopted the cult of "hard dry things," but Hulme and his friends believed in limiting form and matter principally as a matter of literary discipline. And by re-embodying actual personages within the requirements of a strict form, whether rimed or unrimed, Pound experienced the same degree of discipline: both methods were equally valid escapes from "the 'cosmic' crowd."

In *The Spirit of Romance* and in the introduction to his Cavalcanti Pound asserted the criteria of Hulme: in the former he emphasized the precision of Daniel and Dante as opposed to the rhetoric of Milton, and in the latter he wrote that "the rhythm of any poetic line corresponds to emotion. It is the poet's business that this correspondence be exact, i.e. that it be the emotion which surrounds the thought expressed." [42] Since he had already practiced these beliefs in his poetry, I think we may be sure that Pound arrived at them independently, though per-

haps the wording of the second statement is
due to Hulme. "Le fond engendre la forme
comme la tortue ou l'huître l'écaille et la
nacre de sa carapace ou de sa coquille,"
Remy de Gourmont had already written,[43]
and Hulme knew Gourmont thoroughly.

When, in 1912, Pound started to read the
modern French writers, it was with strictly
practical intentions: he knew a certain
amount about technique; he was given to
understand they had faced the very problems now before him; he wanted to see what
they had to offer. He saw in them the first
vital advance since Villon. After reading
and imitating the "Litanies" of Gourmont,
Pound wrote:

> I suppose M. De Gourmont knows more about
> verse rhythm than any man now living; at least
> he has made a most valuable contribution to the
> development of the strophe. It seems to me the
> most valuable since those made by Arnaut Daniel,
> but perhaps I exaggerate.[44]

This represented a snap judgment which
Pound later modified, but it shows his approach to the new literature. Now, quite as
much as when he first joined Flint and Hulme,
Pound judged the new poetry in terms of the

old. Or, rather, he fitted both new and old into one pattern. The finest minds can synthesize experiences, but Pound's is that lesser type of mind that imposes a mould on his experiences, forcing different materials into the same pattern. His pattern here is that of technique. But while we may regard it as a limitation in Pound's interests or understanding that he considers master-writers only those people who "invent" some literary form, it is at least a consistent and coherent limitation, and one which he understands both by instinct and experience. It is only later when Pound imposes on nonliterary experiences other moulds which he does not understand so well, or when he leaves his experiences undigested, that we feel he is bewildered and hence bewildering.

M. Taupin has pointed out the French influence in *Ripostes* (1912); it worked mostly in perfecting Pound's sense of the strophe.[45] "Apparuit" is not a concentrated poem; Pound shows in it a new development of his sense of color ("Golden rose the house. . . . Crimson, frosty with dew. . . . Green the ways . . ."), but his color sense is not frozen into any one picture; it moves from form to

[33]

form. The French influence manifests itself
in perfecting the equilibrium of the strophes
in which these forms move, and here Taupin
sees the general influence of Gourmont,
though not the imitation of any particular
poem. "The Alchemist," on the contrary, is
almost a *pastiche* of Gourmont's "Litanies."

"The Return," perhaps the most perfect
poem Pound has ever written, crystallizes
his knowledge of the strophe. It is modeled
on the introductory poem to Henri de Régnier's "Médailles d'Argile" [46] and has the
same tempo as the French poem. Pound
cuts his lines at the same intervals, and uses
the same sort of expression and repetition:

> See, they return, one, and by one,
> With fear, as half-awakened;
> As if the snow should hesitate
> And murmur in the wind,
>   and half turn back . . .
>
> Une à une, vous les comptiez en souriant,
> Et vous disiez: il est habile;
> Et vous passiez en souriant.[47]

But Pound, as M. Taupin has shown, has
been selective rather than imitative: out of
several rhythms used by Régnier he has
taken only one, and achieved a perfect unity.
It is truly a lovely thing:

See, they return; ah, see the tentative
Movements, and the slow feet,
The trouble in the pace and the uncertain
Wavering!

See, they return, one, and by one,
With fear, as half-awakened;
As if the snow should hesitate
And murmur in the wind,
                    and half turn back;
These were the "Wing'd-with-Awe,"
                    Inviolable.

Gods of the wingèd shoe!
With them the silver hounds,
                    sniffing the trace of air!

Haie! Haie!
          These were the swift to harry;
These the keen-scented;
These were the souls of blood.

Slow on the leash,
                    pallid the leash-men!

This poem, dating six months after "Apparuit," took Pound only fifteen minutes to write. I think there could be no more perfect example of the sudden fruition of long study and much thought.

In two other important poems Pound shows how he has absorbed the past into something that is quite his own. "The Seafarer" is a perfect re-creation of the Anglo-

Saxon poem and, with its rough stern beauty, it is, as Eliot says, so far from being a mere *tour de force* that it opens a new development in alliterative verse.[48] And "A Virginal" shows how Pound can and will, at any time, turn back from new rhythm to the sonnet form whenever he has a thought that naturally shapes itself as a sonnet. This sonnet, with its exclusively feminine rimes, has caught the imaginative coloring of Provence, especially in the last lines, but it has also the French clarity that Flint had been hammering into Pound.

The poems in *Ripostes* show Pound drawing nearer his contemporaries. "N. Y." has the cadences of the whole group, and the overpraised "A Girl" has something of H. D. in it, though not her best. Pound is working to compress his emotion to a single image presented in a single flash, but he does not often succeed in this first "modern" book. One obvious way to achieve concentration is by working at epigrams, and Pound is mildly successful from the start. A mild epigram is not very much use in itself, but as training it has a purpose, and his study was soon to bear fruit.

V
IMAGISM AND THE CAMPAIGN

Pound knew less about French literature than Flint, but he could more easily synthesize what he knew, and because he was more dogmatic in his judgments he came to replace Flint as propagandist of French literature in London.[49] Similarly, though he had not read the rather difficult French literature that sought the Nature of the Symbol, his formula, "An 'Image' is that which presents an intellectual and emotional complex in an instant of time," [50] is a brilliant statement of the result of Hulme's reading and thinking. Hulme was never a propagandist, and by 1912 he had decided he was not a poet. The publication of "The Complete Poetical Works of T. E. Hulme" (five poems) at the end of *Ripostes* marked Pound's taking over the leadership of the group. And by saying, in his introduction to Hulme's poems, "As for the future, *Les Imagistes*, the descendants of the forgotten school of 1909, have that in their keeping," [51] Pound gave the new school a name that now appears inevitable.

Flint, in his studies in French literature, had written of "Neomallarmisme," "Unanimisme," "Paroxisme," "Impulsionnisme," and "Futurisme," and Pound felt that where there were so many schools "Imagisme" had as much right to a credo as any. He, Richard Aldington, and H. D. found they were agreed on three principles:

1. Direct treatment of the "thing" whether subjective or objective.

2. To use absolutely no word that does not contribute to the presentation.

3. As regards rhythm: to compose in the sequence of the musical phrase, not in the sequence of a metronome.[52]

These principles were printed in *Poetry: A Magazine of Verse* for March, 1913, and were followed by "A Few Don'ts by an Imagiste" signed by Ezra Pound. He started with the formula he had derived from Hulme, and then said "It is better to present one Image in a lifetime than to produce voluminous works." This is the statement of an ideal toward which Pound was consciously striving, but which he had only occasionally achieved. The "Don'ts" that follow are interesting as rules of thumb which he had derived from his own work. I select:

THE POETRY OF EZRA POUND

Use no superfluous word, no adjective, which does not reveal something.

Don't use such an expression as "dim lands *of peace.*" It dulls the image . . . the natural object is always the *adequate* symbol.

Go in fear of abstractions.

Don't imagine that the art of poetry is any simpler than the art of music.

Let the candidate fill his mind with the finest cadences he can discover, preferably in a foreign language,* so that the meaning of the words may be less likely to divert his attention from the movement.

It is not necessary that a poem should rely on its music, but if it does rely on its music that music must be such as will delight the expert.

Let the neophyte know assonance and alliteration, rhyme immediate and delayed, simple and polyphonic, as a musician would expect to know harmony and counterpoint and all the minutiae of his craft. No time is too great to give to these matters or to any one of them, even if the artist seldom have need of them.

In short, behave as a musician, a good musician, when dealing with that phase of your craft which has exact parallels in music.

Consider the definiteness of Dante's presentation as compared with Milton's rhetoric. Read as much of Wordsworth as does not seem too unutterably dull.

If you want the gist of the matter go to Sappho, Catullus, Villon, Heine when he is in the vein, Gautier when he is not too frigid; or, if you have

---

* This is for rhythm, his vocabulary must of course be found in his own native tongue. (Pound's note)

not the tongues, seek out the leisurely Chaucer. Good prose will do you no harm, and there is good discipline to be had by trying to write it.

Translation is likewise good training.

If you are using a symmetrical form, don't put in what you have to say and then fill up the remaining vacuums with slush.[53]

Of course these maxims are the common sense rules that almost all good poetry has always followed, and there is nothing new in them except the emphasis on music and perhaps the condemnation of Milton. But although they seem commonplace now, they were important, first, because Pound practiced them himself, and second, because they very definitely needed saying at the time he said them. "Nineteen-twelve was a bad year," wrote Pound looking back from 1915, "we all ran about like puppies with ten tin cans tied to our tails. The tin cans of Swinburnian rhyming, of Browningisms, even . . . of Kiplingisms, a resonant pendant, magniloquent, Miltonic, sonorous." [54]

Pound's assumption of the leadership of the Imagistes marks the beginning of what we may call his "period of influence." Poetically he was quite formed; after this he undergoes new influences but they are only modifications and developments of characteristics in *Personae* and *Ripostes*. Now for the first time he takes the position of leader of poets and dictator to men. Long ago Whitman had proclaimed that great poetry requires great audiences, and it was Hulme's opinion that though Romanticism was actually dead the critical attitude appropriate to it still hung on. Speaking of modern critics, he said:

> The dry hardness which you get in the classics is absolutely repugnant to them. Poetry that isn't damp isn't poetry at all. . . . Verse to them always means a bringing in of some of the emotions grouped round the word infinite.[55]

Pound wanted to wake up poets and hearers at once, both in England and America. His first opportunity came in America; Harriet Monroe had sensed the restlessness under the surface of American letters, and *Poetry: A Magazine of Verse*, established in October, 1912, gave an outlet to the new current. Pound appeared in the first issue, with a poem, "To Whistler, American" arraigning his country for inhospitality to the arts.[56] He was immediately named foreign correspondent of the magazine and from then on

the Imagistes had an American public.
Miss Monroe says:

> It was due more to Ezra Pound than to any
> other person that "the revolution" or "the ren-
> aissance," or whatever one chooses to call the
> freer modern impulse in poetry, was on. Thus,
> without slurring the quality of his poetry, one
> may admit that most people who have watched
> the course of this impulse think of Ezra Pound
> first as a force. If, as Carl Sandburg said . . .
> "he has done most of living men to incite new
> impulses in poetry," the reason is not only the
> lithe *insouciance* of his verse, but still more the
> ardent professorial rage in him — the love of
> stirring up and leading forth other minds.[57]

And in spite of their subsequent feud Amy
Lowell always insisted on Pound's ability to
stimulate. "He could *make* you write," she
would say.[58]

Within two years Amy Lowell, Robinson
Jeffers, Edgar Lee Masters, Edna Millay,
Sara Teasdale, and Vachel Lindsay published
in America: aside from the thin and little-
known volumes of E. A. Robinson it was the
first crop of real poetry for two generations.

Free verse did not take hold in England
the way it did in America, although there
too Pound influenced the tone of a periodi-
cal. It was originally a suffragist organ called

The New Free Woman; after seven months of
Pound it became *The Egoist.*

Early in 1914 *Des Imagistes: An Anthology*
appeared in England and America, edited by
Pound. He, Aldington, H. D., and Flint
were featured, while seven other poets including Amy Lowell were represented by one
poem apiece. Miss Lowell resented being
used, as she thought, for padding, and felt
that for her own literary dignity she must
either be in or out.[59] In the ensuing fracas
it is hard to distinguish whether she bolted
with the group or Pound bolted from it, but
the result was that she published the three
successive anthologies with the name "Some
Imagist Poets," the "Some" and American
spelling "Imagist" leaving the way open for
Pound to do as he pleased. Pound said he
couldn't accept certain people as his critical
and creative equals, and promptly styled
himself a Vorticist.

It is extremely hard to differentiate between the literary aspect of Vorticism and
Imagisme: both use H. D.'s "Oread" as
their typical poem, though the Vorticists,
feeling that life should be lived in the present,
leave off the classical title. The real differ-

[43]

ence between the two seems to be that Imagisme is purely literary, while Vorticism embraces all the arts, holding that

'Every concept, every emotion, presents itself in some primary form. It belongs to the art of this form.' . . . The Vorticist uses the 'primary pigment.' Vorticism is art before it has spread itself into flaccidity, into elaboration and secondary applications.[60]

But Imagisme is obviously the literary expression of those thoughts which present themselves as word-pictures, and all Pound's determination to call the two movements by different names does not change the fact that they are one and merely results in an humiliating muddle: "The Image is not an idea. It is a radiant node or cluster; it is what I can, and perforce must call a VORTEX." [61] And that is that.

Of course this example of bluffing and bullying his way through a muddle is interesting chiefly for the light it throws on his poetry. A man's thoughts or feelings cannot possibly remain parceled off in tight compartments of his mind, and all this turmoil does come out later in Pound's poetry. He had become permeated with the sense of "the public" and his relation to it; he did not try to make poems out of the clashing of cliques, but he did present the problem of the artist against society.

> As bright white drops upon a leaden sea
> Grant so my songs to this grey folk may be

prayed Pound in the first poem in his first book. But now he is more militant:

Go, my songs, to the lonely and the unsatisfied,
Go also to the nerve-wracked, go to the enslaved-
by-convention,
Bear to them my contempt for their oppressors . . .
Go to the bourgeoise who is dying of her ennuis,
Go to the women in suburbs . . .
Go to the adolescent who are smothered in
family —
Oh how hideous it is
To see three generations of one house gathered
together!
It is like an old tree with shoots
And with some branches rotted and falling.[62]

Twelve of the seventy-seven poems in *Lustra* are addressed directly to, or are directly about, his poems. Most of them were written around 1912–1913; many of them appeared in *Poetry* during 1913. They were fighting years, and it was a worthy cause,

but whatever excuse there is for propaganda-
prose I cannot see any for propaganda-
poetry. Poetry about poetry ("Chapman's
Homer" included) is never very interesting *as
poetry*, regardless of its value as biography
or criticism; poetry about the poetic impulse
can occasionally be very charming, but poetry about the poetic mission, however pret-
tily or vigorously elaborated, is usurpation.
It does not fit in with any scheme or school,
though it is nearer the class of "cosmic emotion" than the class of small dry things; it is,
in fact, simply a case of the advertising agent
embezzling the funds that were meant for
production.

Of course writing in 1913 about 1913 is one
way of being up-to-date, but Pound had not
been medieval in writing about Piere Vidal
and Bertran de Born and Arnaut of Marvoil.
He was as thoroughly convinced of their life
as of his own. As Eliot says,

Pound is often most 'original' . . . when he is
most 'archaeological.' . . . If one can really pene-
trate the life of another age one is penetrating the
life of one's own. . . . The people who tire of
Pound's Provence and Pound's Italy are those
who cannot see Provence and medieval Italy except as museum pieces. . . .[63]

[46]

and Pound's own words, speaking nominally of Vorticism, say much the same thing.

> I began this search for the real in a book called *Personae*, casting off, as it were, complete masks of the self in each poem. I continued in a long series of translations, which were but more elaborate masks.[64]

Conversely, he will not necessarily grasp the true life in modern living simply because he makes epigrams on Chesterton, societ·· lawyers, society marriage, adultery, promiscuity, or a new chop-house. These poems are not meant to be profound, but epigrams should at least be penetrating, or so brilliant on the surface that they seem so. But Pound's "Meditatio" is representative of all his squibs:

When I carefully consider the curious habits of
    dogs
I am compelled to conclude
That man is the superior animal.
When I consider the curious habits of man
I confess, my friend, I am puzzled.

Eliot sees poems of this type as exercises in which the poet, lacking a profound emotion or thought, sharpens his talent and keeps it fit for such time as his emotion will be crystallized.[65] And Pound may be thinking of this sort of poem when he says that one cannot get a vortex into everything one does. But in reading his satires I think we cannot help suspecting that he does not have very much to say. Give him the skeleton of another age and he can breathe life into it, but give him the flesh and blood of his own age and he cannot find the skeleton. He covers his lack of critical intelligence by a continual polishing of technique, and by an increasing dogmatism. His words are becoming more and more precise, and he marks this change in himself by setting aside his old poems and their admirers:

> You were praised, my books,
> because I had just come from the country;
> I was twenty years behind the times
> so you found an audience ready.
> I do not disown you,
> do not you disown your progeny.
>
> Here they stand without quaint devices,
> Here they are with nothing archaic about them.
> Observe the irritation in general.[66]

This precision manifests itself when Pound treats again some of his old Provençal themes, taking them out of the realm of song

[48]

and putting them into a new kind of poetry
that had to be brought to the level of the
prose of Flaubert and Maupassant. Some
time before the end of 1908 he had written:

> Pass I on
> Unto Lady "Miels-de-Ben,"
> Having praised thy girdle's scope
> How the stays ply back from it;
> I breathe no hope
> That thou shouldst . . .
>   Nay no whit [67]

Six years later he wrote:

> I of Miels-de-ben demand
> Her straight fresh body,
> She is so supple and young,
> Her robes can but do her wrong.[68]

I think there is a loss here, but in "Provincia
Deserta," another poem in *Lustra*, Pound
atones by recounting his walks through a
country that was now his own by actual as
well as imaginative experience.

> I have walked
>   into Perigord,
> I have seen the torch-flames, high-leaping,
> Painting the front of that church;
> Heard, under the dark, whirling laughter . . .
> I have seen the fields, pale, clear as an emerald,
> Sharp peaks, high spurs, distant castles.

"Whirling laughter" is the suggestive, trans-
sensuous sort of epithet Pound had noticed

in Yeats,[69] and shows how the influence of the older poet was still working in him, if only subconsciously and much changed. There is genuine feeling here. Pound had grown sick of his satires. With:

> Your emotions?
> Are those of a maître-de-café

he tosses them aside in his "Epilogue" just as he had tossed aside his medïeval canzoni to welcome the satires, and all English poetry to welcome the canzoni. His three "progress" poems, "Anima Sola" (*A Lume Spento*), "Salutation the Second" (*Lustra*), and "Epilogue" (*Lustra*) are really in themselves a history of Pound as poet.

His main interest now is in visual precision, and he is working at once toward concreteness and brevity. Ever since 1909 Pound, as we know, had associated with artists who saw the possibilities in the *tanka* and *haikai*. By 1914 he had read the Japanese Noh plays and was much impressed by the fact that a whole play could consist of a single image.[70] Later he was to translate these plays; for the present he was impressed with their conciseness and applied the lesson to shorter poems. "In a Station of the

[50]

Metro" is as short and vivid as anything
could be:

> The apparition of these faces in the crowd;
> Petals on a wet, black bough.

But this brevity was not effortless, and I
think the story of how the poem took shape
is illuminating:

> Three years ago in Paris I got out of a "metro"
> train at La Concorde, and saw suddenly a beauti-
> ful face, and then another and another, and then
> a beautiful child's face, and then another beauti-
> ful woman, and I tried all that day to find words
> for what this had meant to me, and I could not
> find any words that seemed to me worthy, or as
> lovely as that sudden emotion. And that evening
> . . . I found suddenly the expression . . . not in
> speech but in little splotches of colour. It was
> just that — a "pattern" or hardly a pattern if by
> pattern you mean something with a "repeat" in
> it. But it was a word, the beginning, for me, of a
> new language in colour.
>
> I wrote a thirty-line poem, and destroyed it be-
> cause it was what we call work of the second in-
> tensity. Six months later I made a poem half that
> length; a year later I made the following hokku-
> like sentence.

This account is doubly interesting, for in
addition to showing the artist's blue pencil
it gives the lie to Vorticism.[71] Pound could
not use the "primary pigment," color, but

only the pigment of which he was master, words.

I think this poem alone is sufficient to show that his Chinese translations may be considered "original" and judged by the standards of creation. Eliot, from first hand information, explains the relation of the translations to *Lustra*:

Inasmuch as "Cathay" . . . appeared prior to "Lustra," it is sometimes thought that his newer idiom is due to the Chinese influence. This is almost the reverse of the truth. The late Ernest Fenollosa left a quantity of manuscripts including a great number of rough translations (literally exact) from the Chinese. After certain poems subsequently incorporated in "Lustra" had appeared in "Poetry," Mrs. Fenollosa recognized that in Pound the Chinese manuscripts would find the interpretor whom her husband would have wished; she accordingly forwarded the papers for him to do as he liked with. It is thus due to Mrs. Fenollosa's acumen that we have "Cathay"; it is not as a consequence of "Cathay" that we have "Lustra." [72]

In the Chinese poems Pound's sense of the right word — the word that is imaginatively as well as intellectually inevitable — reaches its climax. According to Fenollosa's essay on "The Chinese Written Character as a Medium for Poetry," Chinese characters are poetic because they are at once concrete and active. "Spring," for example, is represented by "the sun underlying the bursting forth of plants." [73] It was Pound's good fortune to receive the poems in their literal state, and his virtue is that he recognized the rightness of the poems as they stood. His wording, as Eliot says, is absolutely ready for this new impact; the language of "Provincia Deserta" is precisely that of the "Lament of the Frontier Guard."

A gracious spring, turned to blood-ravenous
    autumn,
A turmoil of wars-men, spread over the middle
    kingdom,
Three hundred and sixty thousand,
And sorrow, sorrow like rain.
Sorrow to go, and sorrow, sorrow returning.

But if we think the words, the meter, and the mood are too much Pound and too little Rihaku (Li Po) we have only to look at the "River Merchant's Wife," who is certainly no reflection of Pound's ordinary self.

While my hair was still cut straight across my
    forehead
I played about the front gate, pulling flowers.
You came by on bamboo stilts, playing horse,
You walked about my seat, playing with blue
    plums.

And we went on living in the village of Chokan:
Two small people, without dislike or suspicion. . . .
At sixteen you departed,
You went into far Ku-to-yen, by the river of
    swirling eddies,
And you have been gone five months.
The monkeys make sorrowful noise overhead.
You dragged your feet when you went out.
By the gate now, the moss is grown, the different
    mosses,
Too deep to clear them away!

Turning from this exquisite piece to the poems that appeared in *Blast* during 1914, the contrast between Pound's mastery of the past, when he has an artistic form to guide him, and helplessness in the present, when he has not, becomes painfully apparent:

A little BLACK BOX contains them.
            So shall you be also,
You slut-bellied obstructionist,
You sworn foe to free speech and good letters,
You fungus, you continuous gangrene.[74]

Jean de Bosschère says of poems of this type that "Pound has experience of the Philistines who read his verses. Real pain is born of their stupid interpretation. . . ." [75] That may well be, but the pain is the yowl of an angry bull, not the "Energy of a discriminating element" as his fellow vorticist,

[54]

Wyndham Lewis, claimed.[76] Pound is never very skilful as a satirist, either in the early *Ripostes* and *Lustra* poems or the "Moeurs Contemporaines" sequence of 1915, but like Dr. Johnson, "there is no arguing with him, for when his pistol misses fire, he knocks you down with the butt end of it." His defenders maintain, again, that work of this sort was necessary, that it was the beginning of a period when his statement, "Something has got to be done, or we'll all of us be suppressed" [77] was not mere hysteria. D. H. Lawrence's *Rainbow* was suppressed, Joyce's *Portrait of the Artist*, appearing serially in the *Egoist* was blacked out, parts of *Blast* were blacked out. Pound was influential in fighting this tyranny of the public conscience partly because he was naturally a fighter, and partly because, as an American, he had not yet been called upon to make the world safe for democracy. There was still time for poetry, and in 1916 there were those to whom the name of Pound meant more than that of Joffre.[78] He received, commented on, criticized, and blue-penciled tons of manuscript (Eliot has called Pound the greatest critic with a blue pencil who ever lived); [79] he

[55]

went over the corrected manuscripts, and forced the best of them on not too willing editors.[80]

It is the story of a busy and useful life. Pound had worked hard to clear away mental hazards in poetry; he had taught himself and then others to hear new music, and find new ways of expressing it. It is just one more step to turn on the public and make them accept this serious work of serious artists. He was convinced that "For the arts to exist the attic must be cheap, and the daily salt bread must be cheap. A man must be independent at small cost, and he must have with his indigent independence the *entrée* to the best intellectual company." [81] Pound must have written hundreds of articles from 1912 to the present; some trivial, some merely polemic, some (written directly about, or for, artists, or on some subject he knew thoroughly) of permanent value. But while we may now take the *Blast* poems and later the hell cantos as evidence of letting off inevitable and worthy steam, it does not make them good poetry nor even — alas — good propaganda. Pope learned long ago that the way to defeat your opponent is to make him wish he had never been born, not to make him think he is facing a roaring madman. Perhaps I am dwelling longer on this matter than seems necessary here, since the vituperative poems are few in number, but I am doing it deliberately as a foundation for the *Cantos*. For the *Cantos*, which seem largely obscure or obscene, and sometimes both, have been called sudden madness, and I am convinced that there is little in them which does not grow out of Pound's earlier interests and attitudes.

VI

PROPERTIES AND MAUBERLEY

Between the blasts and the *Cantos* Pound
wrote two important sequences. "Homage
to Sextus Propertius" has been used to
"prove" Pound a charlatan. Scholars who
disliked his early work could only sputter
"but is it art?" (which it practically always
was), but here some obvious mistakes in
translation gave them a rod with which to
attack Pound. It does not matter in the
least that Pound's Latin is not reliable; the
misfortune is that some of his readers once
studied Propertius in school, or have read
him with a scholarly bias. Men like Professor Hale, besides knowing that "canes"
means "thou shalt sing" as well as "dogs,"
have an academic conception of Propertius
which is outraged by Pound's debonair criticism.[82] Pound has always, in a sense, been a
hit-and-run translator: he strikes his object
with a thud, but the picture he carries away
springs from his own sensation, not from the
physical reality of the object. The difference
is that instead of leaving his victim dead on
the road Pound generally brings it to life.

Here the "mistakes" and the "flippancies" are perfectly consistent both with each other and with the poet. Propertius is the most carefully delineated mask that Pound ever made of himself.

"Propertius," written in long loose strophes, was published in 1917. In the ten years since Pound started writing, *vers libre* had developed from an exotic French term, to an appellation used by the Imagists to describe the most exact sort of writing where "the heart is the form," [83] and had then degenerated in other hands to a mechanical shredding of prose. Robert Frost, who was for a time close to Pound, said that his friend had an extraordinary capacity for making poets out of little or nothing.[84] This capacity was probably good for the men, but it had an unfortunate aspect for poetry, as these writers chose free verse only because it looked easy. Pound's own free verse had never been a "runnin' dahn th' road"; he probably knew more about form than any living poet, and, as Eliot said, "no *vers* is *libre* for the man who wants to do a good job." [85] Feeling the thrust of each word as an entity, Pound could not endure their prostitution in padded clichés, but he never claimed that *vers libre* was the only path of salvation. We have seen that he himself uses the sonnet where it "belongs." He had kept his perspective through contact with music and musicians; from Arnold Dolmetsch he learned that *vers libre* had existed in classical music, and that "it is perfectly obvious that art hangs between chaos on one side and mechanics on the other." [86]

But in 1918 Pound and Eliot felt that a more apparent discipline was needed in poetry, and they set the example by bringing over into English the trim stanzas of Gautier. To neither of these men did their quatrains represent any new discipline; Pound's development as a conscious artist also profited Eliot. But, especially in the case of Pound, the innocent, clipped little rimed strophes of *Hugh Selwyn Mauberley* look like a return to strict form from which he had actually never departed. This united front was certainly one factor in the general return to form,[87] but apart from any significance as literary history the poems have great value as biography and poetry. The convictions of Pound about his own age, ineffectual as satire, are biting when presented directly. A decade of London has passed through him; *Mauberley* is his farewell to the age and the place:

> All things are a flowing,
> Sage Heraclitus says;
> But a tawdry cheapness
> Shall outlast our days.[88]

In this sequence Pound has reached a point in compression that Eliot also reached, where an allusion, either in or out of quotation marks, sharpens the message and brings another world to bear on this one. Both use clichés to epitomize a mood, a trick that would have had no meaning except for their long war on the cliché.

It is rather cruel to compare this excellent sequence with Eliot's *Waste Land*, for until such a comparison is made Pound's poems seem clearly conceived, mentally as well as visually, and expressed with concentration. They are. The difference is, that though Pound is closer to Eliot here than at any other time, he has not Eliot's creative imagination, Eliot's fusing intellect, nor Eliot's sense of values. *Hugh Selwyn Mauberley* must, as a whole, be compared to the whole of *The Waste Land*, for the one is as much Pound's farewell to his "botched civilization" as the other is Eliot's to his "unreal city," but I shall try to compare the parts of *Mauberley* to the poems of Eliot written more nearly at the same time.

> The tea-rose tea-gown, etc.
> Supplants the mousseline of Cos,
> The pianola "replaces"
> Sappho's barbitos [89]

is an excellent, even exquisite statement, but

> Gloomy Orion and the Dog
> Are veiled; and hushed the shrunken seas;
> The person in the Spanish cape
> Tries to sit on Sweeney's knees [90]

is drama. Eliot is superior because he can dramatize, and Pound cannot. Even in his "dramatic monologues" the drama yields to the monologue; Pound is a master at catching vocal inflections, but each monologue consists of one voice telling one story, and the emphasis is on the actor and his speech, not on the conflict of emotions the actor describes. In this passage, of course, there is no effort to dramatize.

Pound's lack of dramatic imagination is but one phase of a more fundamental differ-

ence between him and Eliot. When Pound
makes one age show up another, as in the
passage last quoted, it is because of what we
know intellectually to be true of the ages,
but Eliot, "the intellectual poet," works
differently.

> The horses, under the axletree
>   Beat up the dawn from Istria
> With even feet. Her shuttered barge
> Burned on the water all the day.
>
> But this or such was Bleistein's way:
>   A saggy bending of the knees
> And elbows, with the palms turned out,
>   Chicago Semite Viennese.[91]

There is a wealth of emotional suggestion
here that goes far beyond the fact, the picture, or the drama. Pound felt the desic-
cation of modern life quite as strongly as
Eliot, but not so sharply, nor could he realize
its implications so broadly. It is entirely a
matter of thinking and feeling, and not at all
of expression. Pound could express anything he felt. Neither his visual perception
nor his mental conception is in general
superlative, but given the things that are
seen, his visual expression is perfect (*Cathay*)
and given the structure he can evolve a con-

sistent philosophy (Propertius). But given simply a full-hearted, sincere and lasting hatred of post-war England, "an old bitch gone in the teeth," [92] it was beyond him to equal

"That corpse you planted last year in your garden,
"Has it begun to sprout? Will it bloom this year?
"Or has the sudden frost disturbed its bed?
"Oh keep the Dog far hence, that's friend to men,
"Or with his nails he'll dig it up again!" [93]

It is the lack of a piercing and fusing power that prevents even the few pages of *Hugh Selwyn Mauberley* from hanging together, so that the combined impact is not appreciably stronger or more illuminating than the parts. These poems, his only direct literary autobiography, are Pound's one successful attempt at "original" work, in the conventional sense. So far as their reputation is concerned, it is a pity that Eliot wrote a farewell to the same age and place, for the same reasons. But Pound praised *The Waste Land* with characteristic generosity, saying that Eliot had done perfectly what he himself had been trying to do all his life.[94]

VII

THE CANTOS

As we step from *Mauberley* to the *Cantos* it is hard to discover the relation of the two in Pound's mind. It would be expedient to say that after writing his epitaph Pound wished to gather his experiences as a form of testament, but that oversimplifies the situation. Drafts of the earliest cantos appeared three years before the publication of *Mauberley*.[95] It is likely that he saw them as a vast new literary adventure, rather than as a gathering-in of his word-hoard. Pound has always, and justly, considered himself a literary pioneer, and perhaps he felt that the time had come to break new ground. But I think we shall have to see the *Cantos* as a combination of new and old: he shows no new power, but there are new manifestations of the old.

Many modern writers who have incorporated their experience in a longer work have felt the need of a scale of values, a normative conception corresponding, perhaps, to ancient mythology, by which a work can be judged. Eliot has said,

The only way of expressing emotion in the form
of art is by finding an 'objective correlative'; in
other words, a set of objects, a situation, a chain
of events which shall be the formula of that *particular* emotion; such that when the external facts,
which must terminate in sensory experience are
given, the emotion is immediately evoked.[96]

Joyce uses such a correlative in *Ulysses*, and
O'Neill in *Electra*. With Eliot the matter is
more involved. It is apparent, as Matthiessen says, that Eliot relies on "a set of objects" to thread together the range of his
associations.[97] But Eliot uses compressed
references to various myths standing for
fixed values rather than an expanded reference to one myth. His use of the correlative
is complex; Joyce's and O'Neill's simple.
Pound falls between these two uses. He has
chosen two themes, and from different
sources. The plan, as Yeats understood it
from Pound in 1928, is as follows:

It will, when the hundredth Canto is finished,
display a structure like that of a Bach fugue.
There will be no plot, no chronicle of events, no
logic of discourse, but two themes, the descent
into Hades from Homer, a metamorphosis from
Ovid, and mixed with these medieval or modern
historical characters. He has tried to produce
that picture Porteus recommended to Nicolas

[66]

Poussin in "Le Chef d'Oeuvre Inconnu" where everything rounds or thrusts itself without edges, without contours — conventions of the intellect — from a splash of tints and shades, to achieve a work as characteristic of the art of our times as the painting of Cézanne . . . a poem in which there is nothing that can be taken out and reasoned over, nothing that is not a part of the poem itself. He has scribbled on the back of an envelope certain series of letters that represent emotions or archetypal events — I cannot find any adequate definition. A B C D and then J K L M and then each set of letters repeated and then A B C D inverted and this repeated and then a new element X Y Z and then certain letters that never recur and then all sorts of combinations of X Y Z and J K L M and A B C D and D C B A and all set whirling together. He has shown me upon the wall a photo of a Cosimo Tura decoration in three compartments, in the upper the Triumph of Love and the Triumph of Chastity, in the middle Zodiacal signs, and in the lower certain events in Cosimo Tura's day. The descent and the metamorphosis — A B C D and J K L M — his fixed elements, took the place of the Zodiac — the archetypal persons — X Y Z, that of the triumphs, and certain modern events — his letters that do not recur — that of the events in Cosimo Tura's day.[98]

Such is Yeats's story of Pound's plan. But is seems to me that such an outline, no matter how faithfully followed, would not lend intelligibility to a poem because the

[67]

pattern elements do not stand for anything but themselves. There is little use in calling some events "eternal" and some "recurrent" if, at best, none of them can be taken out and reasoned over. Yeats concludes his account on a note of hope:

> I may, now that I have recovered leisure, find that the mathematical structure, when taken up into the imagination, is more than mathematical — that seemingly irrelevant details fit together into a single theme, that there is no botch of time and colour . . . except where one discovers beautiful detail. . . .

I can offer no such hope. I cannot pretend to see the *Cantos* as Pound sees them; I can only see them as I see Pound.

I see Pound as a craftsman, a man who, first and foremost, is a specialist in words and metrics. He has never been successful in building a coherent whole out of his words and music, but in the early poems this is no defect, for they have either stood alone as musical gems or have relied on an outside structure, and he has been so successful as musician and translator that we seldom realize his limitation as thinker.

It is far more apparent in his prose. Pound has written a great deal of literary criticism

that is valuable, for the writing of a specialist
is always valuable, but once he steps beyond
the question "what has this man achieved
technically" he is lost. He cannot and will
not examine a man coolly or with any pre-
tense of a system. His method is that of a
restless and absent-minded autocrat who
quotes favorite passages, comments spon-
taneously and, it often seems, irrelevantly,
and then throws the book at you with all his
force saying sweetly "this is really going to
do you a lot of good." We may accept his
word where he has proved his mastery; there
is little reason why we should in other fields.
Yet even in his *A B C of Economics* he boasts
that "I am not proceeding according to
Aristotelian logic but according to the ide-
ogramic method of first heaping together the
necessary components of thought." [99] His
thoughts on economics are not important for
the early cantos, but his presentation in this
"brief formal treatise" is most illuminating.
Here his avowed purpose is "to express the
fundamentals of economics so simply and
clearly that even people of different economic schools and factions will be able to
understand each other when they discuss

[69]

them." [100] Our professor of French clarity then wallows in titles that have nothing to do with their chapters, and chapters without titles, repetition of favorite phrases, italics, capitalizations, bold faced type, and lists in which only the numbers show a discernible sequence. It is mumbo-jumbo criticism of the worst sort in which the author, scorning persuasion, tries to hypnotize and overwhelm his public.

When Pound is not poet and aesthete he seems always to be a bully. The method of Pound the economist is the method of the man who flew into big black print over Vorticism, and the man whose "satire" consisted almost entirely of abuse. In every case he has covered a lack of perception by a torrent of dogmatism. One cannot help being suspicious of oratory; it may be justified for soapbox consumption, where the orator has to make himself heard above all distractions, but you cannot bludgeon a reader into accepting your printed word: the essence of reading is reflection. Pound will not admit this. He has always been contemptuous of the public intelligence: "What the public wants is ME" he once told Ford Madox

Hueffer, "because I am not an imbecile like the component members of the public." [101] But another public figure has said that you can't fool all of the people all of the time.

Lacking a mentally intelligible form to impose upon the *Cantos* from without, and incapable of erecting a structure from within, Pound could save his cantos from chaos only by holding to a fixed and communicable scale of values for touchstones. But here we see his greatest failure: Pound has no scale of values. He very seldom passes judgment outside his field of aesthetics and when he does the judgment is of the most obvious kind. His mind is not big enough to include anything but technique, and all his sallies outside of "art" have been to secure an orderly world where the artist may function, not as "seer blest" but as the inventor of language. He is made frantic by the politicians, the profiteers, and the obstructors of knowledge who will not keep the possessors of genius immune from the slow contagion of daily life, and from its disastrous combustions. He resents the war, not as the tragedy of our civilization, but as an unpardonably stupid intrusion of the world on the artist.

And Henri Gaudier went to it,
      and they killed him,
And killed a good deal of sculpture,
And ole T. E. H. he went to it,
With a lot of books from the library,
London Library, and a shell buried 'em in a dug-
    out,
And the Library expressed its annoyance.[102]

It has been a long time since prevalent literary opinion has felt that artists, as a caste, would save the world, but most artists today feel that they are at least citizens of the world, and that however they choose to act they must at least think in terms of the problems of good and evil around them. Eliot, no social reformer, is his own Tiresias and has foresuffered all, and it is because he at once participates in our futility and recognizes its ugliness by inflexible standards of good and evil that his work has tragic dignity. But Pound has neither standards nor sensibility, and therefore the *Cantos* have neither dignity nor unity: nominally he uses a correlative, but instead of being simple or complex it is merely complicated.

Eliot says that this complication does not bother him; he is convinced that Pound thinks he has a plan, and that is enough.[103]

This seems clearly the defense of the friend rather than the judgment of the critic, but of course it may well be said that Pound is not aiming at a logical straight-ahead structure, but at the far more complex problem of interrelating the "ideograms" of his mind. The trouble is that they do not interrelate. It is Pound's tragedy that his medium is words, for in the *Cantos* his very service to language has undone him. He had been so fundamentally stirred by the Chinese vision of the word as picture, which filled out Hulme's concept of the physical reality of words, that he did not realize that in anything larger than one brief image words must have mental significance as well as physical. As R. P. Blackmur says:

It is irrelevant to speculate as to the possible success of an ideographic method applied to ideographic symbols; Mr Pound has not made that experiment. He has proved, rather, the impossibility of combining an ideographic structure and a language whose logic is verbal without to a considerable extent vitiating the virtues of both.[104]

Pound uses verbal expressions as though they were phrases in music; there seems to be a deliberate confusion of the technique of the two arts. Because of this confusion one canto seldom illuminates the next. The only value of reading them as a whole is for the shock of juxtaposition, of passing from the Honest Sailor to Kung and his Dynastic Temple, and thence to Hell. Pound knows a variety of things, and with his old trick of style and vision is still

Suddenly discovering in the eyes of the very beautiful Normande cocotte
The eyes of the very learned British Museum assistant,[105]

but the result is not an increased sense of values where the cocotte, the Museum assistant, past, present, heaven, and hell mean more to us than ever before, but simply a confused and continuous present where the world is so full of a number of things that we all have as many papers to go through as kings. Everything Pound handles he does with zest and vigor, but the piling up of fact on fact or fancy on fancy more often creates an accelerated, almost nightmare impressionism, than a concentrated image. I feel the effect is too vague to have significance, but perhaps this is what Pound meant by having everything "round and thrust itself without edges, without contours."

The *Cantos* are not important as a unified
judgment of life, or even as a portrayal of
life, and Pound's talk of "eternal values"
is just talk, but if we strip his "plan" of
everything that does not appear in the cantos, and the cantos of everything that does
not appear in the plan, there is a thread of
method in the madness. I think, however,
that critics have made an unfortunate mis-
take in treating the *Cantos* as if each series
were a separate book, to be judged by standards of unity, dignity, and intelligibility.
Pound has persistently refused to write his
memoirs, and the reason may be that all his
interests and experiences find a direct, rather
than a sublimated, expression in his writing.
The *Cantos* are not one book, or two or three
books, they are his intellectual diary from
1915 to this day, with reminiscences of everything that has interested him before he
started them and hints of his preoccupa-
tions in the future. If considered as an or-
ganic growth, large, rambling perhaps, and
certainly uneven, but a dynamic rather than
a static mass, they do cohere, and in running
rapidly over them I shall try to distinguish
the traces of Pound's plan and the more

[75]

significant order that the cantos possess as mental autobiography.

At first his postulated plan is discernible; he translates the descent into Hades from Divus's Latin version of Homer, and then slips into a metamorphosis from Ovid. Thus his chosen themes are established in the first two cantos and associated by the words

And poor old Homer blind, blind, as a bat,
Ear, ear for the sea-surge, murmur of old men's
  voices

which appear in the beginning of the Ovid section. By persistently blending Helen of Troy and Eleanor of Aquitaine in a rather beautiful confusion, Pound is enabled to pass from Greek myth to Provençal romantic history, and as he passes back and forth he touches momentarily on Piere Vidal, Pieire de Maensac, and other characters who appeared at greater length in his *Personae*. Most of the subject matter of these early cantos is not new to Pound; it is in blending the tales that he experiments. Pound holds together the different ages, characters, and episodes in this first section by a skilful use of the imagism of water, the formless and all-containing element. Odysseus goes over the

sea before his descent, and the Metamorphosis takes place on a ship bound for Naxos.
In these first two cantos the ocean is the scene
of action: in the following three water is used
as the atmosphere, implicit in the third and
fourth cantos, briefly explicit in the fifth:

> 'Came lust of woman upon him,'
> Poicebot, now on North road from Spain
> (Sea-change, a grey in the water)
> And in small house by town's edge. . . .

In addition to the leveling quality of water
Pound evokes its coolness and its magic
quality of reflecting deep and solid objects
only as fluid and fragmentary images. This
very skilful use of water, and to some extent
air, in imagery is something to which Pound
frequently reverts in the later cantos when
he wants to transmit echoes of an unreal
past. But he never overdoes the symbolism,
which is absent in the matter-of-fact sixth
canto, only to be reiterated in his "Poor old
Homer" refrain in the seventh:

> Ear, ear for the sea-surge;
> rattle of old men's voices.

The substitution of "rattle" for "murmur"
is significant; it marks Pound's leaving the
world of romance for the realism of history.

[77]

If we could pretend that Pound's Renaissance figures are medieval, as they are historical, his plan would still be visible in the second section of his *Cantos*. His Malatesta, Sforza, Este, and Medici, who seem to be his "archetypal forms" are certainly intended as foils for his modern characters and "events that do not recur." He does not mean them to appear romantic, and burrows into documents to make the period seem a sordid mass of political intrigue and puppet-warfare. These cantos have been much criticized, and they are exasperating. Pound transcribes phrases, summarizes some incidents and hints at others, but he tells little in full that seems related to anything else he tells. "Confusion," as Blackmur has observed, "is . . . a deliberate element of procedure, but its success . . . will depend on how well the things confused are known." Here, "it is not the meaning but the very subject of the thing that must be hunted down" and "Thus the poem is either lost in the original or becomes an attachment to it: is scholia not poetry." [106] Pound's discussion of Renaissance intrigues is rather like the conversation of one's elders: at first it sounds exciting because it seems to hint at so much, but when we know the whole story it proves just more talk.

Pound's Renaissance cantos are at once bewildering and disappointing because he has no artistic model for his historical characters, and history, unless seen with perspective, is formless, so that the Malatesta of the documents clutters up Pound's imagination till the Italian is neither himself nor a mask of Pound. This brings Cantos VIII–XI in line with all of Pound's previous work, which has always proved disappointing when he had no artistic model to serve as his scaffold. But in these cantos the confusion is deliberate: he reduces his heroes to midget-size and tumbles them around without ceremony to prepare us for their modern counterparts. He knows that they are nothing but Mexican beans jumping in meaningless confusion; to emphasize this point he flashes in Canto XII a picture of order and magnitude that is his ideal, and which, appearing just after his prelude to modern times is placed in apposition to both the fifteenth and twentieth centuries. Then, after we have drawn our breath with Confucius, Pound tosses us into the center of his modern hell where all the people he hates most are suffering the most loathsome fates he can devise for them. But although he means his hell cantos to be a panorama of vermin, because that is how he sees the betrayers of language and other profiteers, he does not convince, he merely disgusts us. Both the Renaissance and the hell sequences fail as poetry because they make their subject matter seem unimportant: in a human drama there cannot be an unending procession of villains and they cannot be beans or flies. Because his characters have, by definition, no tragic dignity, Pound's hell is, as Matthiessen calls it, journalistic, "a hell" (here he quotes Eliot) "for the *other people*, the people we read about in newspapers, not for oneself and one's friends." [107] Pound is vivid enough, but when we compare his laboriously accumulated filth with Eliot's stark "That corpse you planted last year in the garden," we see the difference between a mind that hates and abuses and a mind that is horrified and can symbolize its horror in one unforgettable image. A river of water and disinfectant would wash away Pound's hell;

Eliot's contagion is in the marrow of civilization.

So far traces of Pound's original plan have been visible, if only as a casual use of two themes and a playing off of "medieval" and modern characters. Cantos I–XVI, summarizing Pound's literary interests before 1914 and his reaction to the war, were published in 1925. But from the time we leave Hell Mouth in Canto XVI, no amount of simplification can make the cantos adhere to the plan, unless we decide that this is the place where all the elements are set whirling together. In this new series we move forward with Pound himself, and I think the only sequence these cantos possess is the "post" or "propter" of his interests.

We know from *Mauberley* and the hell cantos that the horror and stupidity of war impressed Pound, and in Canto XVIII he reiterates his disgust:

War, one war after another,
Men start 'em who couldn't put up a good hen-
    roost.

The trend of Cantos XVIII–XXX, in so far as they have one trend, is an examination of business and a survey of the men who start

and profit by war. We have had preludes to
both subjects in the earlier cantos, but now
Pound inspects his principal villains, and his
work becomes more interesting as he tells
their stories instead of smearing them with
vituperation. In these cantos the refrain is
no longer "Poor old Homer . . ." but

> An' that man sweat blood
> to put through that railway,
> And what he ever got out of it? [108]

and the conclusion seems to be

'Nothing we made, we set nothing in order . . .
'We have gathered a sieve full of water.' [109]

In addition to the unscrupulous financiers,
munitions-makers, oil-men, and railway
magnates, Pound indicts our stupid econ-
omists:

And C. H. said to the renowned Mr Bukos:
'What is the cause of the H. C. L.?' and Mr
    Bukos,
The economist consulted of nations said:
            'Lack of labour.'
And there were two millions of men out of work.
And C. H. shut up, he said
He would save his breath to cool his own porridge,
But I didn't, and I went on plaguing Mr Bukos
Who said finally: 'I am an orthodox
'Economist.'
            Jesu Christo! [110]

Pound's exclamation comes from the heart. Three cantos earlier some one had said of a coal mine:

> Run it, of course we can run it,
> We can't sell the damn coal.

Recognizing that improper distribution of wealth rather than underproduction of goods is responsible for our economic troubles, Pound has now turned to Social Credit as the panacea, and had made it one of the main themes in Cantos XXXI–XLI. Those who have known him only by his early poems are surprised at this, but it is a natural outgrowth of his post-war confusion. Pound has never been concerned with bettering the condition of poor people as people, but he has always resented his own poverty and that of his fellow artists with whom he has habitually shared his last sixpence. And now, realizing that for artists to exist at all there must be a degree of stability in the world, that

A decent concept of a twentieth century world is like a decent concept of a town or a family, you don't want your neighbour down with cholera; you don't want your family full of sickly members all yowling for help,[111]

[83]

he grasps at Major Douglas's plan because it claims to eliminate poverty without organizing the masses, and who else can create Eden with a calculating machine? And so Pound has put aside the work he understands to go stumping for Social Credit, and has made a number of very poor cantos out of the Bank War.

But the New Economics is not the whole story of the new Pound, for, much to the distress of Major Douglas, Pound sees in Fascism the political counterpart of Social Credit. All his life, as I have repeatedly stated, he has needed a form through which to express himself, and now that he has abandoned order in art he seems to have found his personal correlative in Mussolini's Italy. He styles himself a disciple of Confucius, and sees in Il Duce a man who has order in himself and is spreading order around himself. But while the introduction of Mussolini into his saga in Canto XLI forms an amazing parallel to the flash of Kung in Canto XIII, the resemblance cannot have been present in Pound's mind when he wrote the earlier canto, for in those days Mussolini was just another Italian to him.[112]

So that the semblance of plan given the *Cantos* by the parallelism between the old and new order, as the old and new chaos, was unpremeditated, though it is very welcome.

It is the more welcome because Cantos XVII–XLI contain a vast jumble of material to which I have not even referred in following the trend of Pound's new interests. Stories of Odysseus, Sigismundo, the Medici, Sordello, snatches of his own experiences in Freiburg and Vienna, sketches of the lady from Topeka and Mrs. Kreffle, all whirl merrily in and out of an increasing haze of material that calls Mussolini's Italy the spiritual descendent of Jefferson's America, and proclaims that only in "l'idea statale" shall we find salvation.

But if they are such a hodge-podge of confused particles that satisfy neither our minds nor our emotions, why are Pound's *Cantos* so fascinating? For they are fascinating, at least to me, or I should never have studied Pound. Blackmur thinks that the very confusion is responsible:

Mr Pound put together the materials and aroused the interests appropriate to a narrative,

[85]

and then deliberately refused the materials a narrative form, without, however, destroying the interests that expected it. Whether intentionally or not, it is the presence of this defeated expectation which holds these cantos together. That is the attraction which the parts exert over each other; an attraction which constantly makes the Cantos seem on the point of re-arranging themselves in an order quite different from the printed order, and quite different, also, from the historical order upon which the printed order is founded. But this third order is not achieved; there is a clog, a stoppage, at the point of crisis, and the Cantos fall back in the dismay of choices that cannot be made. Climax, what happens when things meet in a form and have ending, is rejected for the inchoate, the anecdotal, the deliberately confused, a jungle.[113]

This analysis is very shrewd, but I think that when we examine the "interests appropriate to a narrative" we find that in Pound's case it is not so much the stories as the voice telling them that compels our attention. "The cantos are talk, talk, talk," says Allen Tate, "not by anyone in particular to anyone else in particular; they are just rambling talk." [114] And it is because they have caught the accent of speech and seem always about to say something important, although they never say it, that the *Cantos* are so fascinating. Pound is infernally clever with language. At the risk of laboring the point I must insist that for him there are no dead languages, that he rimes Greek and English words in *Mauberley* because he hears, not sees, them, and that from the first his Personae were alive because they used the most colloquial as well as accurate expressions. For him words were never something to be used one way in poetry, another way in prose, and a third way in talking to his friends: all his writing in any one period shows his attitude toward words in that period, and more and more his written word has come to be governed by the inflections of speech. Iris Barry has said that Pound's diction in 1916 was "almost a wholly original accent, the base of American mingled with a dozen assorted 'English Society' and Cockney accents inserted in mockery, French, Spanish and Greek exclamations, strange cries and catcalls, the whole very oddly inflected with dramatic pauses and *diminuendos*." [115] This is not the speech of Pound's early writings, although it grows out of that speech: it is, very definitely, the tone of a great part of the *Cantos*.

[87]

When Pound jibes

Dey vus a bolcheviki dere, und dey dease him:
Looka vat youah Trotzsk is done, e iss
    madeh deh zhamefull beace!!

when he echoes

  'Peace! Pieyce!!' said Mr Giddings,
'Uni-ver-sal? Not while yew got tew billions ov
    money,'
Said Mr Giddings, 'invested in the man-u-facture
'Of war machinery. Haow I sold it to Russia —
'Well we tuk 'em a new torpedo-boat . . .'

when he tells the story of the peautiful chew-
ish poy, and Meestair Freer and the wholley
man; when he makes an Italian war-lord say
"But dey got de mos' bloody rottenes' peace
on us" and an American President proclaim:

Nowhere so well deposited as in the pants of the
    people
Wealth ain't,[116]

Pound is writing as people talk. Each
canto is equal in length to a conversational
thought; the Cantos, the chapters in the
books on economics, his magazine defenses
and his letters all run from two to ten minutes reading time, which may well be the
length of a mood, and Pound shows inordi-
nate skill in making the poetic moods sound
important.

But is this the skill for which we value
Pound? "Anyone can shoot to excess,"
said his Kung in the thirteenth canto. "It
is hard to stand firm in the middle." And in
much of his work since 1915, and most of it
since 1925, Pound has taken from his quiver
the old charge, but shot wide of the mark.
It takes a clear sense of values to stand firm
in the middle, and Pound has no such sense.
Nor has he had the wit consistently to confine himself to forms where his limitation
will not be a defect. When he does so confine
himself, or when he relies on an outer structure, he can still create poems of great
beauty. His superb translation of Homer in
the first canto, the lovely song that opens
the thirtieth canto, and his fine reworking
of Cavalcanti's "Donna mi Priegha" in the
thirty-sixth are examples of his mastery.
With such a power we must regret that he
has made so great a portion of the *Cantos* a
mere *tour de force*, and that a further exaggeration of his talent makes the colloquial
language of his books on economics an insult
to our intelligence.

As a good reader you will refuse to be bam-
boozled, and when a text has no meaning or when

it is merely a mess or bluff you will drop it and occupy yourself with good literature.[117]

Thus in his latest book Pound himself furnishes us an exit tag.

As we leave him in his study at Rapallo, shadowed by documents which dangle from ropes attached to the ceiling, and surrounded by vast portfolios of other material which he wants eventually to incorporate in his cantos,[118] we leave a man who thinks he is working out his destiny as a son of Confucius, who feels that he is furthering the cause of Cosmos against a relapse into Chaos.

But we are also leaving a man who has done more for poetry than almost any of his contemporaries. We may belittle his general ideas; there is no belittling his poetic achievement. Pound entered the service of English letters when the grate was cold. He stirred up the embers of poetry and kindled a flame that has lasted twenty years. If he seems outmoded now it is because the fire no longer needs his care, and he has run off into the night after will-o'-the-wisps.

NOTES

NOTES

Unless otherwise indicated, poems of Pound are included in *Personae: The Collected Poems*, New York, 1926; *A Draft of XXX Cantos*, London, 1933; or *Eleven New Cantos*, XXXI–XLI, New York, 1934.

1. *Selected Poems of Ezra Pound*, London, 1928, p. xxii.
2. "Mea Patria," *New Age*, Sept. 26, 1912. Quoted by René Taupin, *L'Influence du Symbolisme Français sur la Poésie Américaine*, Paris, 1929, p. 7.
3. "Patria Mia," *New Age*, xii (1912), p. 12.
4. *How To Read*, Le Beausset (Var.), France, 1932, p. 7.
5. So he says in *Make It New*, London, 1934, p. 8.
6. *The Spirit of Romance*, London, 1910, p. vi.
7. T. S. Eliot, *Ezra Pound: His Metric and Poetry*, New York, 1917, p. 8.
8. *The Spirit of Romance*, p. 13.
9. *Ibid.*
10. "Anima Sola," *A Lume Spento*, Venice, 1908. wierd (*sic*).
11. "*Salve O Pontifex: To Swinburne; an hemichaunt*," as printed in *A Lume Spento*. Much later he was to write, "She says I used to read Swinburne 'so splendidly!' Damn it! I believe this to be true." *Imaginary Letters*, Paris, 1930, p. 10.
12. *Selected Poems of Ezra Pound*, p. xiii.
13. "Mesmerism."

14. "La Fraisne."
15. *Pavannes and Divisions*, New York, 1918, p. 151.
16. *Make It New*, p. 32.
17. *The Spirit of Romance*, p. 32.
18. *Make It New*, p. 50.
19. *Ibid.*, p. 47.
20. *The Spirit of Romance*, p. 26.
21. *A Lume Spento*, Venice, 1908.
22. Not included in his collected edition.
23. Dedication to *A Lume Spento*.
24. "Alba Belangalis" was published in the Hamilton College Magazine in 1905; "In Durance" is dated 1907.
25. Eliot, *Metric and Poetry*, p. 6.
26. Not included in his collected edition.
27. F. S. Flint, "The History of Imagism," *Egoist*, ii (1915), p. 70.
28. S. F. Damon, *Amy Lowell*, Boston, 1935, p. 203, *note*.
29. Glenn Hughes, *Imagism and the Imagists*, Stanford University Press, 1931, p. 12.
30. *The Spirit of Romance*, p. 18.
31. *Metric and Poetry*, p. 12.
32. He wrote in *Make It New*: "What obfuscated me was not the Italian but the crust of dead English, the sediment present in my own available vocabulary — which I, let us hope, got rid of a few years later. You can't go round this sort of thing. It takes six or eight years to get educated in one's art, and another ten to get rid of that education.

    "Neither can anyone learn English, one can only learn a series of Englishes. Rossetti

made his own language. I hadn't in 1910
made a language, I don't mean a language
to use, but even a language to think in"
(p. 399).

33. *The Spirit of Romance*, pp. 101, 90.
34. *The Sonnets and Ballate of Guido Cavalcanti*,
    London, 1912, p. xvi.
35. "Avete in voi" and "Thy form" are on
    pp. 30 and 31 of the *Cavalcanti*; he reprints
    Cavalcanti's "Donna mi Priegha" in *Make
    It New*, pp. 363–367.
36. Damon, *Amy Lowell*, p. 203.
37. Taupin, *Symbolisme Français*, pp. 84–85.
38. T. E. Hulme, *Speculations*, New York, 1924,
    pp. 131, 132, 136.
39. *Ibid.*, pp. 134–135.
40. Canzo XII, stanza ii, quoted in *Make It New*,
    p. 77.
41. *The Spirit of Romance*, p. 27.
42. *Cavalcanti*, p. xxii.
43. Taupin, *Symbolisme Français*, p. 114.
44. "The Approach to Paris," *New Age*, xiii
    (1913), p. 577.
45. *Symbolisme Français*, pp. 141–142.
46. *Ibid.*, p. 142.
47. *Ibid.*, p. 143.
48. *Metric and Poetry*, p. 17.
49. Taupin, *Symbolisme Français*, p. 139.
50. "A Few Don'ts by an Imagiste," *Pavannes
    and Divisions*, p. 96.
51. *Ripostes*, London, 1912, p. 59.
52. Pound, *Pavannes and Divisions*, p. 95.
    Pound says that the three of them agreed on
    these principles in the spring or early summer

of 1912, but Damon (p. 205, *note*) says that Pound's reference to Flint's article, which Pound misdates, places this formulation later.

53. *Pavannes and Divisions*, pp. 96–101.
54. "Webster Ford," *Egoist*, ii (1915), p. 12.
55. *Speculations*, p. 127.
56. Damon, *Amy Lowell*, p. 206.
57. *Poets and Their Art*, New York, 1926, p. 17.
58. Damon, *Amy Lowell*, p. 208.
59. *Ibid.*, p. 237.
60. Pound, "Vorticism," *Fortnightly Review*, cii (1914), p. 466.
61. *Ibid.*, p. 469.
62. "Commission."
63. *Selected Poems of Ezra Pound*, p. xii.
64. *Fortnightly Review*, pp. 463–464.
65. *Selected Poems of Ezra Pound*, p. xx.
66. "Salutation the Second."
67. "Na Audiart."
68. "Dompna Pois de me No'us Cal."
69. He commented on Yeats's "black wind" (*Spirit of Romance*, p. 167), which he imitates more directly in "black lightning" in "The Spring."
70. "Vorticism," *Fortnightly Review*, p. 471.
71. It appears in his defense of Vorticism, pp. 465 and 467.
72. *Metric and Poetry*, pp. 21–22.
73. Edited by Pound, *Instigations*, New York, 1920, p. 364.
74. "Salutation the Third."
75. "Ezra Pound," *Egoist*, iv (1917), p. 28.

76. Quoted by Carl Sandburg, "Work of Ezra Pound," *Poetry*, vii (1916), p. 257.
77. Iris Barry, "The Ezra Pound Period," *Bookman*, lxxiv (1931), p. 163.
78. *Ibid.*, p. 162.
79. Dr. Theodore Spencer told me of this remark of Eliot's.
80. Iris Barry, "The Ezra Pound Period," p. 163.
81. "Paris Letter," *Dial*, lxxi (1921), pp. 462–463.
82. W. G. Hale, "Pegasus Impounded," *Poetry*, xiv (1919), pp. 52–55.
83. Pound and Fenollosa, *Noh or Accomplishment*, New York, 1917, p. 52. Coming from the Noh plays, this phrase shows how the concept of *vers libre* derived equally from French and Japanese sources.
84. Dr. Spencer told me of this remark of Frost's.
85. *Selected Poems of Ezra Pound*, p. viii (requoted).
86. *Pavannes and Divisions*, pp. 155, 258.
87. In 1931 Pound wrote "Those writers to whom *vers libre* was a mere 'runnin' dahn th' road,' videlicet escape, and who were impelled thereto by no inner need of, or curiosity concerning, the quantitative element in metric, having come to the end of that lurch, lurch back not into experiment with the canzone or any other unexplored form, but into the stock and trade sonnet." *Make It New*, p. 375.
88. *Hugh Selwyn Mauberley*, III.
89. *Ibid.*
90. Eliot, "Sweeney Among the Nightingales," *Collected Poems: 1909–1935*, New York, 1936, p. 65.

91. "Burbank with a Baedeker: Bleistein with a Cigar," *Collected Poems*, p. 47.
92. *Hugh Selwyn Mauberley*, V.
93. *The Waste Land*, I, *Collected Poems*, p. 72.
94. Dr. Spencer told me of this praise.
95. In *Poetry* for June, July, and August of 1917 (x, pp. 113, 180, 248). Most of this material was later discarded.
96. F. O. Matthiessen, *The Achievement of T. S. Eliot*, Boston and New York, 1935, p. 57.
97. *Ibid.*, p. 61.
98. *A Packet for Ezra Pound*, Dublin, 1929, pp. 2-3.
99. London, 1933, p. 37.
100. *Ibid.*, p. 7.
101. Hueffer (Ford Madox Ford), *Thus to Revisit*, London, 1921, p. 140.
102. Canto XVI.
103. "Isolated Superiority," *Dial*, lxxxiv (1928), p. 6.
104. "Masks of Ezra Pound," *Hound and Horn*, vii (1934), p. 209.
105. "Pagani's, November 8." Dudley Fitts, in "Pound and the Cantos," *Saturday Review of Literature*, viii (1931), p. 416, applied this poem of Pound to the author.
106. "Masks of Ezra Pound," pp. 201, 207.
107. *The Achievement of T. S. Eliot*, p. 67.
108. Cantos XXII and XXVIII.
109. Canto XXV.
110. Canto XXII.
111. *Jefferson and/or Mussolini*, London, 1935, p. 75.
112. He says in *Jefferson and/or Mussolini*, pp. 49-51: "... possibly in '21 the cavalieri

della morte passed through the Piazza
San Marco, and when I got to Milan that
year I asked my friend what about it.
What is this fascio? He said there was
nothing to it or words to that effect. At
any rate not a matter of interest.

"You know how it is when you stop off for
a night in a hurry . . . in '21 or '22 or whatever spring it was, I hadn't any excuse save
an interest in other matters and the sup-
position that IF it were interesting my friend
would have known it.

"Life was interesting in Paris from 1921 to
1924, nobody bothered much about Italy."

113. "Masks of Ezra Pound," pp. 199–200.
114. "Ezra Pound's Golden Ass," *Nation,*
cxxxii (1931), p. 632.
115. "The Ezra Pound Period," p. 159.
116. Cantos XVI, XVIII, XXXV, XXII, XI,
XXXVII.
117. *Jefferson and/or Mussolini,* p. 22.
118. Mr. James Laughlin IV described Pound's
study to me.

BIBLIOGRAPHY

BIBLIOGRAPHY

WORKS BY POUND

POETRY

A Lume Spento, Venice, Antonini, 1908.

Personae, London, Elkin Mathews, 1909.

Exultations, London, Elkin Mathews, 1909.

Canzoni, London, Elkin Mathews, 1911.

Ripostes, London, Stephen Swift & Co., 1912.

Personae: The Collected Poems, New York, Horace Liveright, 1926.

A Draft of XXX Cantos, London, Faber & Faber, 1933.

Eleven New Cantos, XXXI–XLI, New York, Farrar & Rinehart, 1934.

PROSE

The Spirit of Romance, London, J. M. Dent & Sons, 1910.

Pavannes and Divisions, New York, Alfred A. Knopf, 1918.

Instigations, New York, Boni & Liveright, 1920.

Indiscretions, Paris, Three Mountains Press, 1923.

Antheil and the Treatise on Harmony, Paris, Three Mountains Press, 1924.

Imaginary Letters, Paris, Black Sun Press, 1930.

How To Read, Le Beausset (Var.), France, 1932.

A B C of Economics, London, Faber & Faber, 1933.

A B C of Reading, New Haven, Yale University Press, 1934.

BIBLIOGRAPHY

Make It New, London, Faber & Faber, 1934.
Jefferson and/or Mussolini, London, Stanley
Nott, 1935.

TRANSLATIONS
The Sonnets and Ballate of Guido Cavalcanti,
London, Stephen Swift & Co., 1912.
Certain Noble Plays of Japan, Churchtown, the
Cuala Press, 1916.
Noh, or Accomplishment (with Ernest Fenol-
losa), London, Macmillan, 1916.
Confucius, Ta Hio, Seattle, University of
Washington Book Store, 1928.

EDITIONS
Poetical Works of Lionel Johnson, London,
Elkin Mathews, 1915.
Active Anthology, London, Faber & Faber, 1933.

ARTICLES IN PERIODICALS
"Patria Mia," *New Age*, xii (1912), p. 12.
"The Approach to Paris," *New Age*, xii (1913),
p. 577.
"Vorticism," *Fortnightly Review*, cii (1914),
pp. 461–471.
"Webster Ford," *Egoist*, ii (1915), p. 12.
"This Constant Preaching to the Mob,"
Poetry, viii (1916), pp. 144–145.
"Island of Paris, a Letter," *Dial*, lxix (1921),
pp. 406–411, 515–518, 635–639.
"Paris Letter," *Dial*, lxxi (1921), pp. 456–463.
"Where is American Culture?" *Nation*, cxxvi
(1928), pp. 443–444.
"Situation," *Poetry*, xxxviii (1931), pp. 95–97.
"Manifesto," *Poetry*, xli (1932), pp. 40–43.

BIBLIOGRAPHY

Works by Others

Damon, S. F., *Amy Lowell*, Boston, 1935.
Eliot, T. S., *Ezra Pound: His Metric and Poetry*, New York, 1917.
—— *Selected Poems of Ezra Pound*, London, 1928.
—— *Collected Poems*, New York, 1936.
Hueffer, F. M. (Ford Madox Ford), *Thus to Revisit*, London, 1921.
Matthiessen, F. O., *The Achievement of T. S. Eliot*, Boston and New York, 1935.
Monroe, Harriet, *Poets and Their Art*, New York, 1926.
Mott, L. F., *The Provençal Lyric*, New York, 1901.
Rossetti, D. G., *Complete Poetical Works* (Translation of Guido Cavalcanti), London, 1882.
Taupin, René, *L'Influence du Symbolisme Français sur la Poésie Américaine*, Paris, 1929.
Waley, Arthur, *A Hundred and Seventy Chinese Poems*, London, 1918.
Yeats, W. B., *A Packet for Ezra Pound*, Dublin, 1929.

Periodical References

M. Bronner, "A Panel of Poets," *Bookman*, xxxv (1912), pp. 156–158.
W. Rice, "Ezra Pound and Poetry," *Dial*, liv (1913), pp. 370–371.
F. S. Flint, "The History of Imagism," *Egoist*, ii (1915), pp. 70–71.
Carl Sandburg, "Work of Ezra Pound," *Poetry*, vii (1916), pp. 249–257.
Jean de Bosschère, "Ezra Pound," *Egoist*, iv (1917), p. 28.

T. S. Eliot, "The Noh and the Image," *Egoist*, iv (1917), p. 102.

"Ezra Pound Crowned," *Literary Digest*, xcvi (1918), pp. 24–25.

J. B. Rittenhouse, "Contemporary Poetry," *Bookman*, xlvi (1918), pp. 577–578.

L. Untermeyer, "Ezra Pound — Proseur," *New Republic*, xvi (1918), pp. 83–84.

W. G. Hale, "Pegasus Impounded," *Poetry*, xiv (1919), pp. 52–55.

M. Sinclair, "Reputation of Ezra Pound," *North American Review*, ccxi (1920), pp. 658–668.

H. S. Gorman, "Bolingbroke of Bards," *North American Review*, ccxix (1924), pp. 855–865.

M. Lesemann, "Mr. Pound and the Younger Generation," *Poetry*, xxx (1927), pp. 216–222.

T. S. Eliot, "Isolated Superiority," *Dial*, lxxxiv (1928), pp. 4–7.

Allen Tate, "Ezra Pound's Golden Ass," *Nation*, cxxxii (1931), pp. 632–634.

Iris Barry, "The Ezra Pound Period," *Bookman*, lxxiv (1931), pp. 159–171.

Mary Moore, "A Draft of XXX Cantos," *Poetry*, xxxix (1931), pp. 37–50.

Dudley Fitts, "Pound and the Cantos," *Saturday Review of Literature*, viii (1931), p. 416.

T. C. Wilson, "Rhythm and Phrase," *Saturday Review of Literature*, ix (1933), p. 677.

C. Aiken, "Personae," *Poetry*, xliv (1934), pp. 276–279.

R. P. Blackmur, "Masks of Ezra Pound," *Hound and Horn*, vii (1934), pp. 177–212.

H. Gregory, "A. B. C. of Ezra Pound," *Poetry*, xlvi (1935), pp. 279–285.